Transportation

El transporte

ehl trahns-*pohr*-teh

Illustrated by Clare Beaton

Ilustraciones de Clare Beaton

BARRON'S

bicycle

la bicicleta

lah bee-see-*kleh*-tah

car

el coche

ehl *koh*-cheh

truck

el camión

ehl kah-mee-*ohn*

boat

el barco

ehl *bahr*-koh

bus

el autobús

ehl ow-toh-*boos*

fire engine

el camión de bomberos

ehl kah-mee-*ohn* deh bohm-*beh*-rohs

motorcycle

la moto

lah *moh*-toh

tractor

el tractor

ehl trahk-*tohr*

digger

la excavadora

lah ex-kah-vah-*doh*-rah

airplane

el avión

ehl ah-vee-*ohn*

train

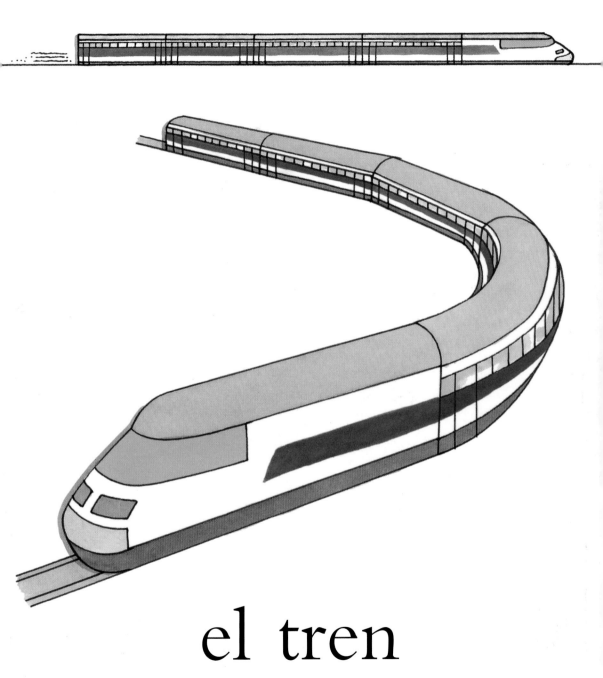

el tren

ehl trehn

A simple guide to pronouncing the Spanish words★

- Read this guide as naturally as possible, as if it were English.
- Put stress on the letters in *italics* e.g. lah *moh*-toh.

la bicicleta	lah bee-see-*kleh*-tah	**bicycle**
el coche	ehl *koh*-cheh	**car**
el camión	ehl kah-mee-*ohn*	**truck**
el barco	ehl *bahr*-koh	**boat**
el autobús	ehl ow-toh-*boos*	**bus**
el camión de bomberos	ehl kah-mee-*ohn* deh bohm-*beh*-rohs	**fire engine**
la moto	lah *moh*-toh	**motorcycle**
el tractor	ehl trahk-*tohr*	**tractor**
la excavadora	lah ex-kah-vah-*doh*-rah	**digger**
el avión	ehl ah-vee-*ohn*	**airplane**
el tren	ehl trehn	**train**

★There are many different guides to pronunciation. Our guide attempts to balance precision with simplicity.

Text and illustrations © Copyright 2002 by B SMALL PUBLISHING, Surrey England.
First edition for the United States, its Dependencies, Canada, and the Philippines published in 2002 by
Barron's Educational Series, Inc.
All rights reserved. No part of this book may be reproduced in any form, by photostat, microfilm, xerography, or any
other means, or incorporated into any information retrieval system, electronic or mechanical, without the written
permission of the copyright owner.
Address all inquiries to: Barron's Educational Series, Inc., 250 Wireless Boulevard, Hauppauge, New York 11788.
(http://www.barronseduc.com)
International Standard Book Number 0-7641-2211-8
Library of Congress Catalog Card Number 2001099159
Printed in China   9 8 7 6 5 4 3 2 1